Begin Sweet World

Photographs by John Pearson

Poetry by Children

Doubleday & Company, Inc.   Garden City, New York

Also by John Pearson: To Be Nobody Else
Kiss The Joy As It Flies
the sun's birthday

ISBN: 0-385-11065-0

Library of Congress Catalog Card Number: 75-9228

All Rights Reserved

Copyright © 1976 by John Pearson
Foreword Copyright © 1976 by Anaïs Nin
Printed in the United States of America

First Edition

Design by Jaren Dahlstrom, Crow-Quill Studios,
San Francisco

First published in 1976 by Doubleday & Company, Inc.

GRATEFUL ACKNOWLEDGMENT IS MADE TO THE
FOLLOWING FOR PERMISSION TO REPRINT:

The poem on page 39 by Melanie Popkin from *Wishes, Lies and Dreams; Teaching Children to Write Poetry* by Kenneth Koch and the Students of P.S. 61 in New York City. Copyright © 1970 by Kenneth Koch. Reprinted by permission of Random House, Inc. and International Creative Management.

The poem on page 73 from "Magic" by Josh in the book *Journeys*, collected by Richard Lewis. Copyright © 1969 by Richard Lewis. Reprinted by permission of Simon and Schuster and Curtis Brown, Ltd.

The poems on pages 6, 9 and 87 by Lynette Joass, page 21 by Susan Morrison, page 28 by Desmond Garton, pages 52, 55, 57 by Vicky Williams, all from the book *Miracles: Poems by Children of the English Speaking World*, compiled by Richard Lewis. Copyright © 1966 by Richard Lewis. Reprinted by permission of Simon and Schuster and Allen Lane, The Penguin Press.

The poem on pages 47 and 50 "Mountains" by Sakai Akiko from the book *There Are Two Lives*, edited by Richard Lewis, translated by Haruna Kimura. Copyright © 1970 by Richard Lewis and Haruna Kimura. Reprinted by permission of Simon and Schuster, Children's Book Division and Curtis Brown, Ltd.

The poem on page 40 from *Photographs and Poems by Sioux Children*, selected by Myles Libhart and Arthur Amiotte. Copyright 1971. Reprinted by permission of the Tipi Shop, Inc., Rapid City, South Dakota.

In Eskimo the word "to make poetry" is the word "to breathe." This book is dedicated to Anaïs Nin for whom poetry has always been as important as breath.

Through familiarity, through accumulation of impressions, our vision of the world around us often grows dim, indifferent, unfocused. The artist and the poet are there to renew this vision, to cleanse our clouded lens, to reawaken the emotion which gave vividness to what we saw. Children possess this clear, transparent and glowing perception, but the poet is the one who in his maturity retains the fresh clear eyes of the child. The child sees everything as new. The illumination of discovery highlights all he observes.

In this book we have the transparency of the children's insight through their poems, their direct and simple statements, their power to infuse all they see with a quality of magic; but we also have the vision of a photographer who has retained all his enthusiasm, his attentiveness, his alertness and responsiveness. With him we rediscover the beauty of a leaf, a tree, a shell, a feather, a sea horse, a rock, a wave, sand, night dreams, hair, vines, the moon.

This vision, so clear in us when we were children, becomes faded and tarnished by preoccupations, contingencies, struggle for survival. Yet it is there in us, and it only takes the time to read these children's poems and to look at the photographs which parallel them, to rediscover and recapture it. John Pearson guides us back to the source of keen pleasure and delight, of early iridescence and contact with beauty.

Anaïs Nin

Dark, dark night.
The trees. The river.
One more day;
For so slow goes the day.
Before the end
   the world goes round
     once more.
The world begins the day.
The night has gone.
The day for the end of the world
   once more begins.
Once more begins the sun
Slow, so slow.
Go on, world, live.
Begin, sweet sun.
Begin, sweet world.
The people live and die.
   people die alive
     alive
       alive.

Lynette Joass
Age 12
New Zealand

The poetry in *Begin Sweet World* is by children from four to fourteen, mostly from the United States. The name, age, and country of each child is given in the back of the book.

The photographs and poems were made independently. Over a period of years I photographed what moved me, and I'm sure the children wrote about experiences and feelings that moved them deeply. Again and again I found poems that expressed my own feelings — and expressed them so simply and beautifully.

As we read these poems from forty-one children, of different ages, backgrounds, and interests, it almost seems as if one child is speaking. The magical thread is the mystery, wonder and delight which all of us feel in the ever changing, ever beginning world of nature.

Begin Sweet World

. . . Once more begins the sun
Slow, so slow.
Go on, world, live.
Begin, sweet sun.
Begin, sweet world . . .

This morning as I was walking
through the woods there was fog
creeping over the trails . . .
It's like walking on clouds
today — it's just one of those
days.

Spring makes everything bloom.
Like God did when the world
was first born . . .

. . . When the robins and all
other birds sing, it makes
you feel alive again.

Color is everything;
Color is the world.
I'm glad I have color.

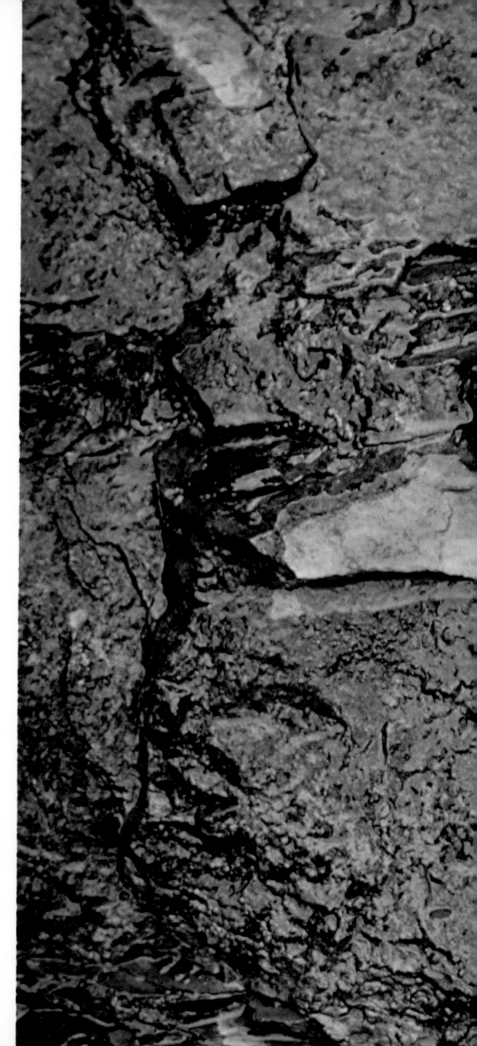

Hours are leaves of life
and I am their gardener . . .
Each hour falls down slow.

A single flower
started all life on
the earth and still
lives today.

**When a flower is finally born
it bursts open with joy.**

Grass is the earth's hair.

Dew is the soft tears
of the glittering moon.

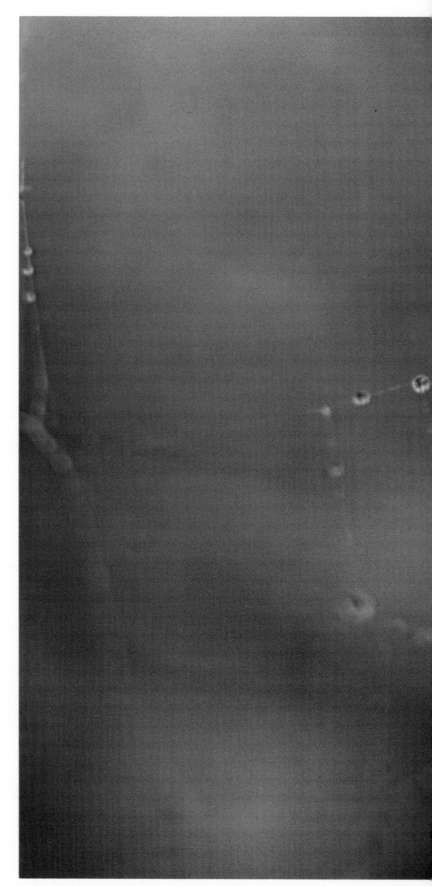

The feather
   in the stillness
That the bird
   left behind.

Snake! Come with me, please. I'll build you a cage so big you'll think you're free. I'll feed you mice three times a week. Snakey, oh snakey, come with me please.

One time I felt as if I could
kiss the whole sky and let all
of the animals out of their cages
and set them free — as free as a
bird whistling through the sky.

35

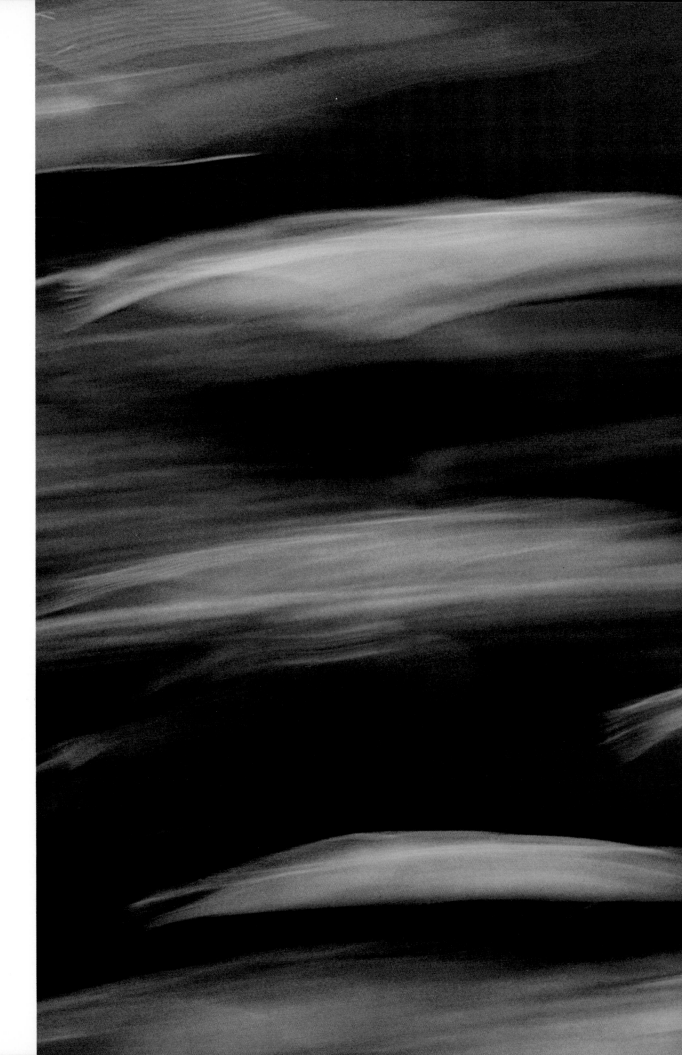

I wish I could leap high into the air
and land softly on my toes.
I wish I could dance in every country
in the world.

If I were a rock
I would be very old
and lie around all day.

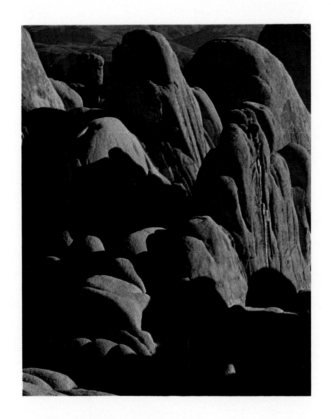

. . . I would be very big
and just lie in the sun
and get warm . . .

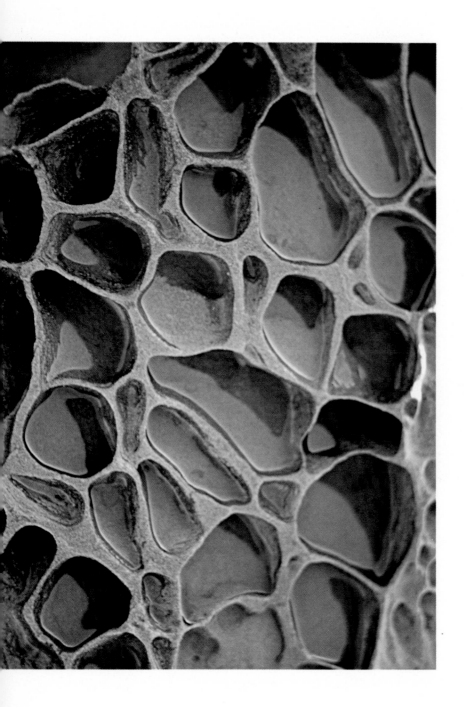

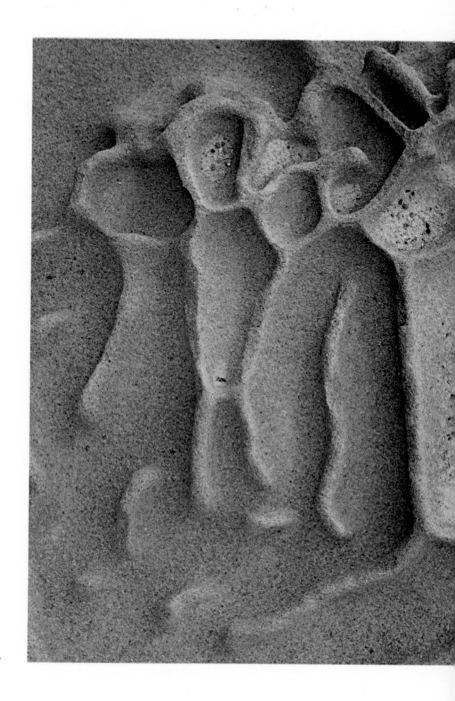

. . . After millions of years I
would have a lot of wrinkles.

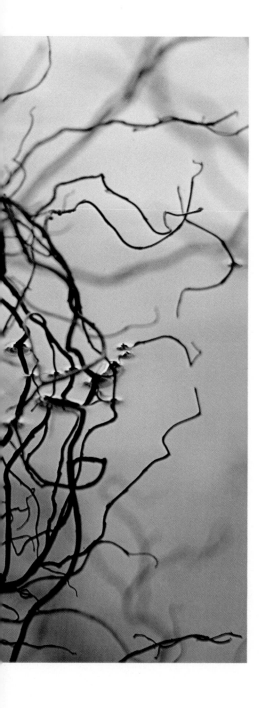

Mountains have nerves.
The roots of trees are
the nerves of mountains . . .

Mountains have ears.
They copy what man says.
Everybody calls it echoes.

...echoes.

A tree is a base for poison ivy.
A tree is a wrinkled old man with
wicked intent, scratching at
windows and scaring babies . . .

. . . A tree is a lady in a new
coat in spring, and nothing in
winter because she wanted too much . . .

56 ... Some trees are non-conformists
but not very many.
A tree is a house where you
don't have to pay any rent . . .

. . . A tree is a place to hide when you want to sulk, where they can't find you. A tree is like an old friend — it grows on you.

The wind is blowing
To help the trees dance.

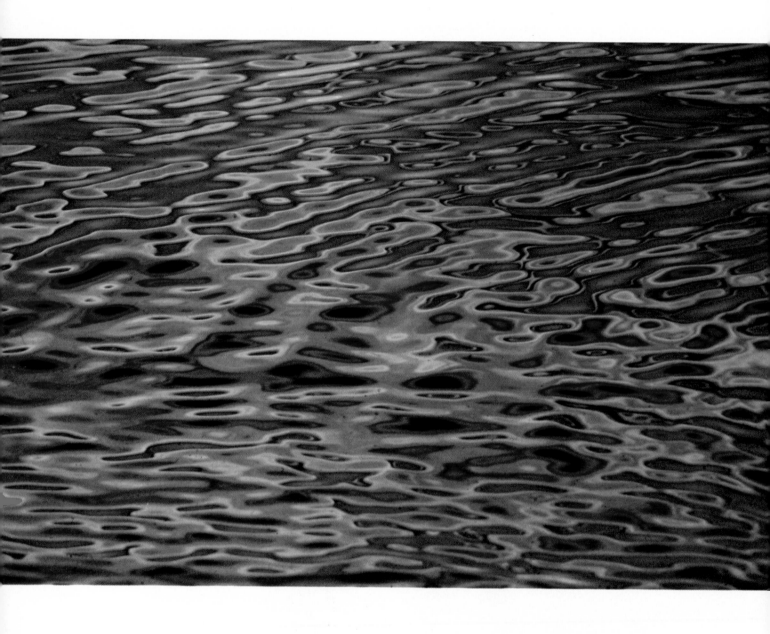

Quietly, softly
the wind blows . . .
Summer day.

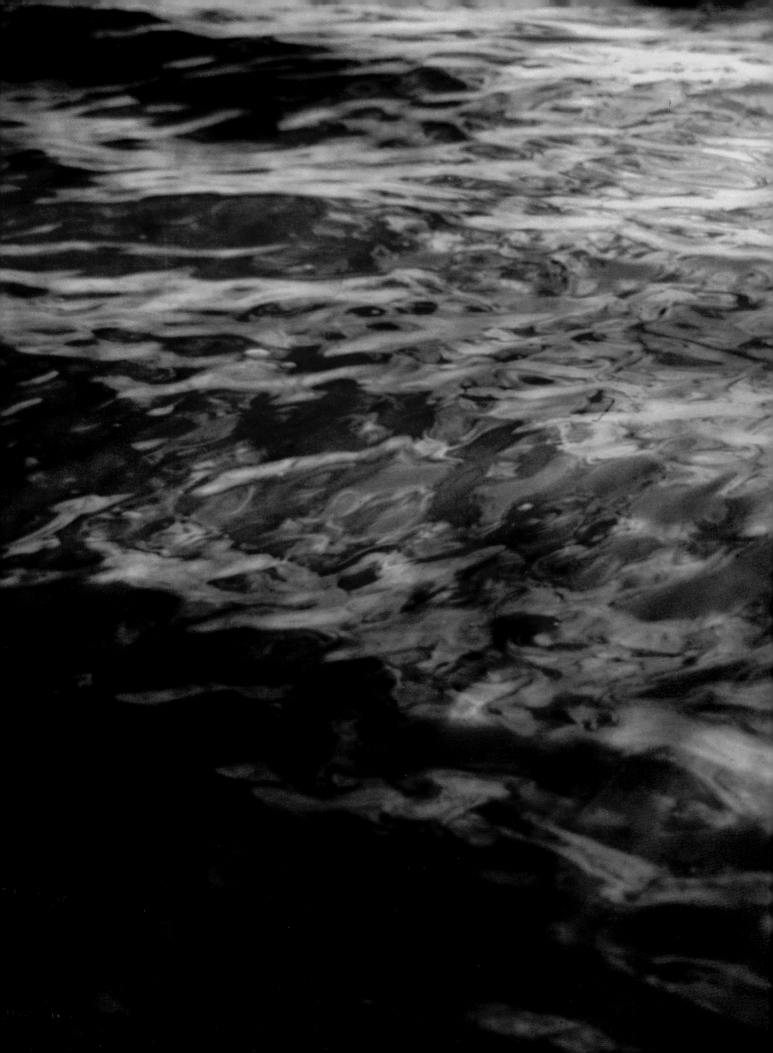

The rain is the tears of a lonely cloud.

**Icicles are the frozen
music of the rain.**

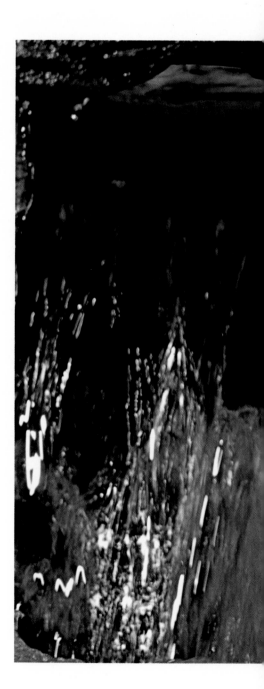

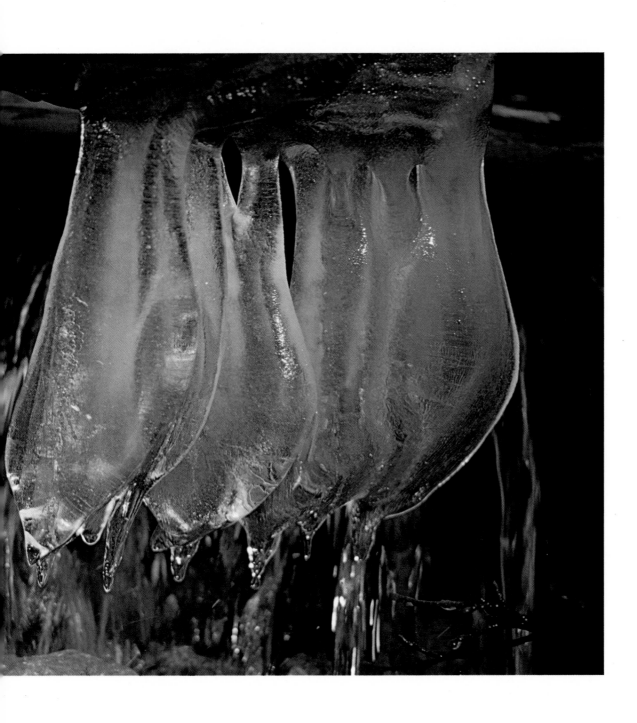

The snow goddess is a beautiful
queen made of ice. Her kingdom is
made of ice — her ice mirror.

Frost is baby snow.

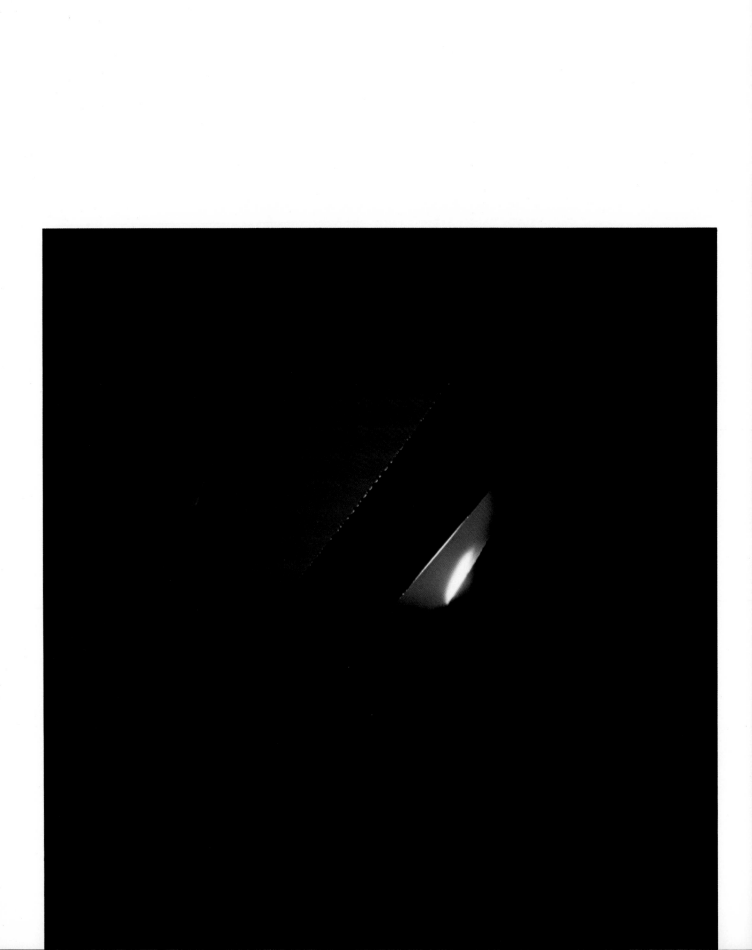

The sky is the sun's blue cape.
But the sun is bashful,
so he hides behind his
black cape until dawn.

I know how daytime changes
into nighttime. Daytime melts.

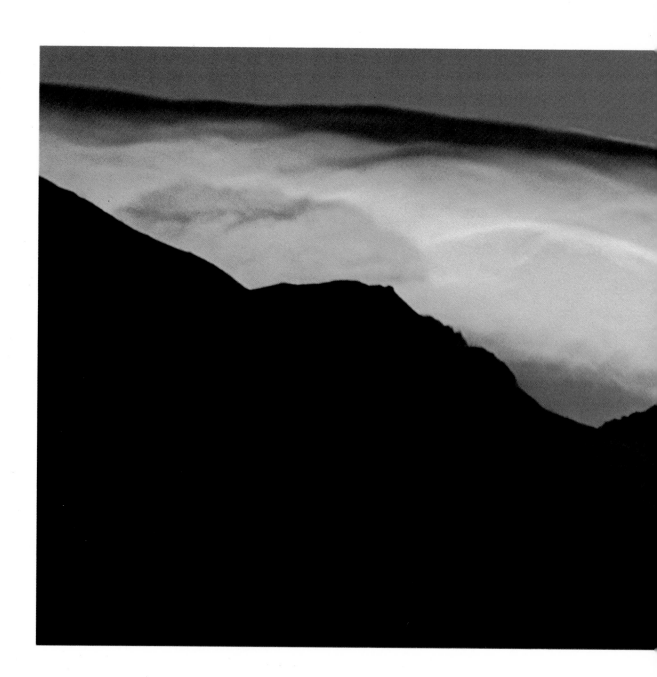

The clouds around the mountains are the gods' blankets.

Night is comfortable to me.
The wind sways slowly,
The moon shines softly,
The bed so warm.

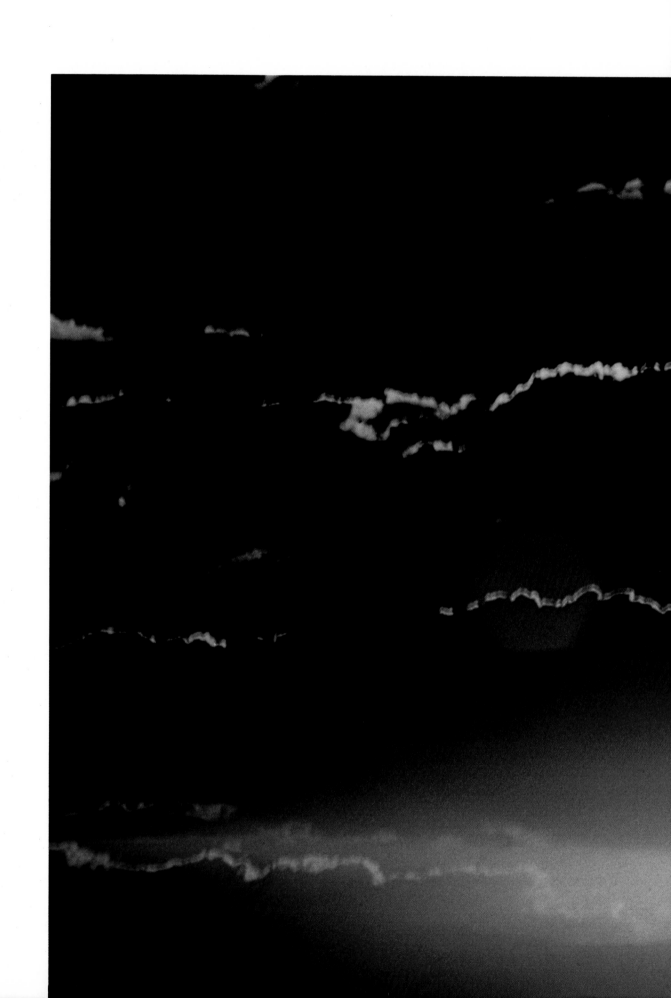

When the gods dance, the sky cracks and
we get a glimpse of the golden heavens.

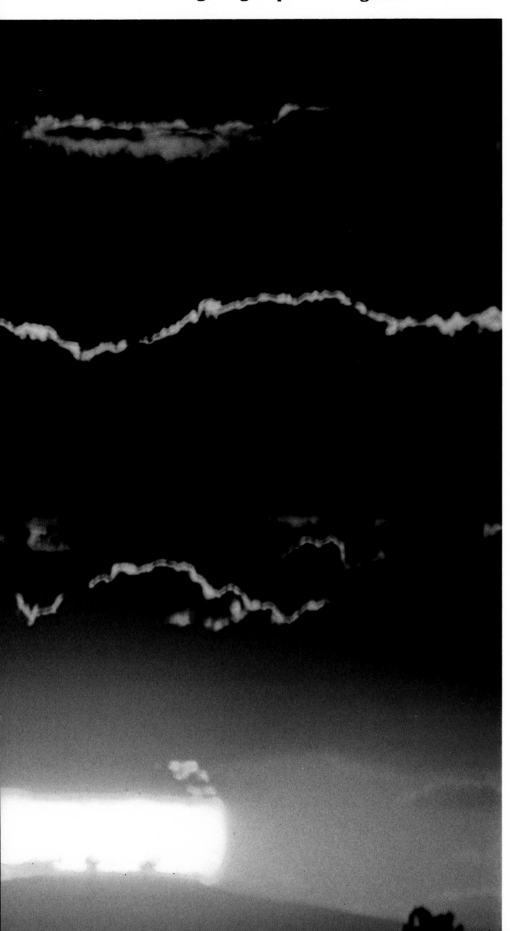

I am the sun
all hot and falling . . .

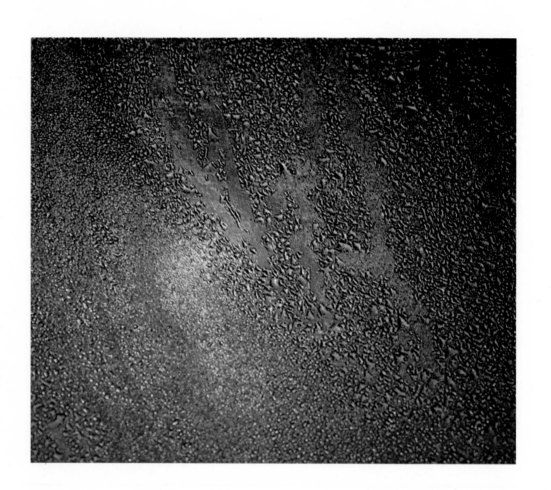

. . . and dancing . . .

...I'm dancing like
them all.

. . . Before the end
    the world goes round
        once more.
The world begins the day.
The night has gone.
The day for the end of the world
    once more begins.
Once more begins the sun
Slow, so slow.
Go on, world, live.
Begin, sweet sun.
Begin sweet world . . .

87

Angels like to celebrate.
They celebrate at night.
Those aren't stars we see
up there. They are the
fireworks of angels.

The big dipper is a container that
is used for holding stars, but every
night it spills them across the sky.
There are so many stars that it takes
all night to pick them up.

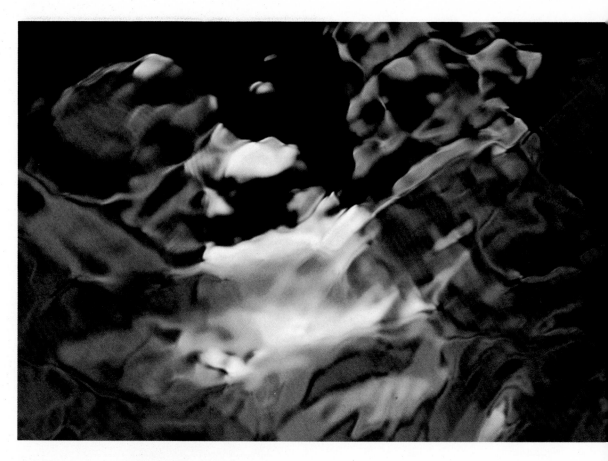

The frog jumped into the moon
and broke it into pieces,
then it spread all over the pond.

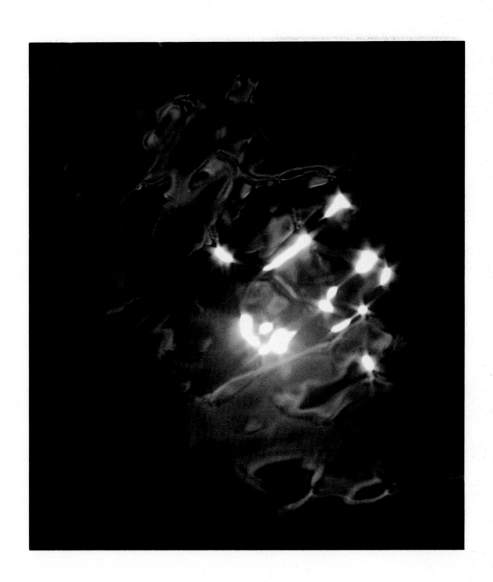

**Some dreams are day dreams,
but my dreams are night dreams . . .**

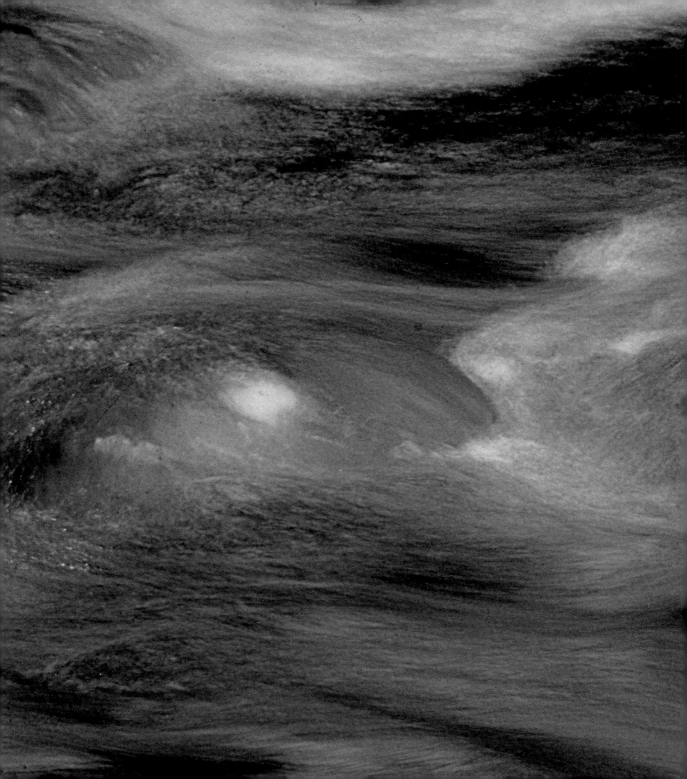

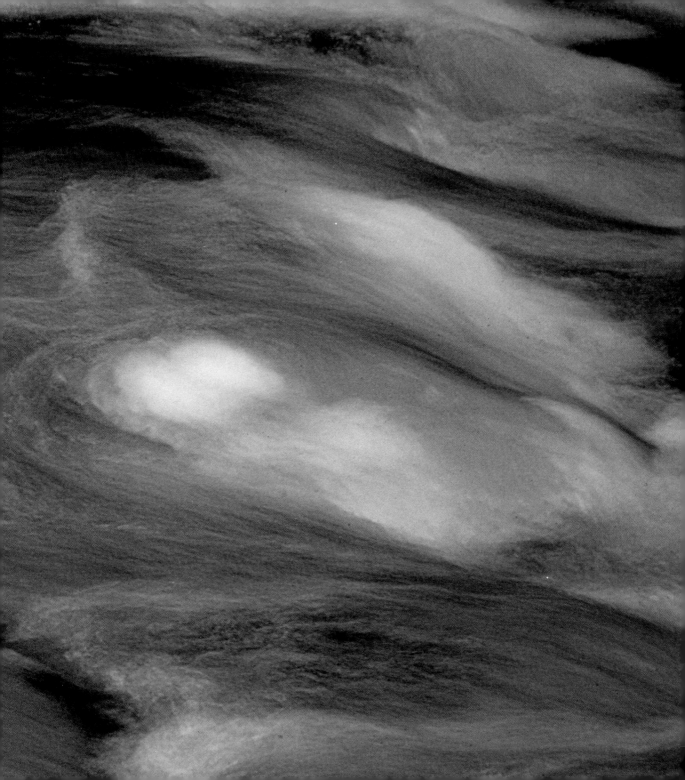

. . . night dreams . . .

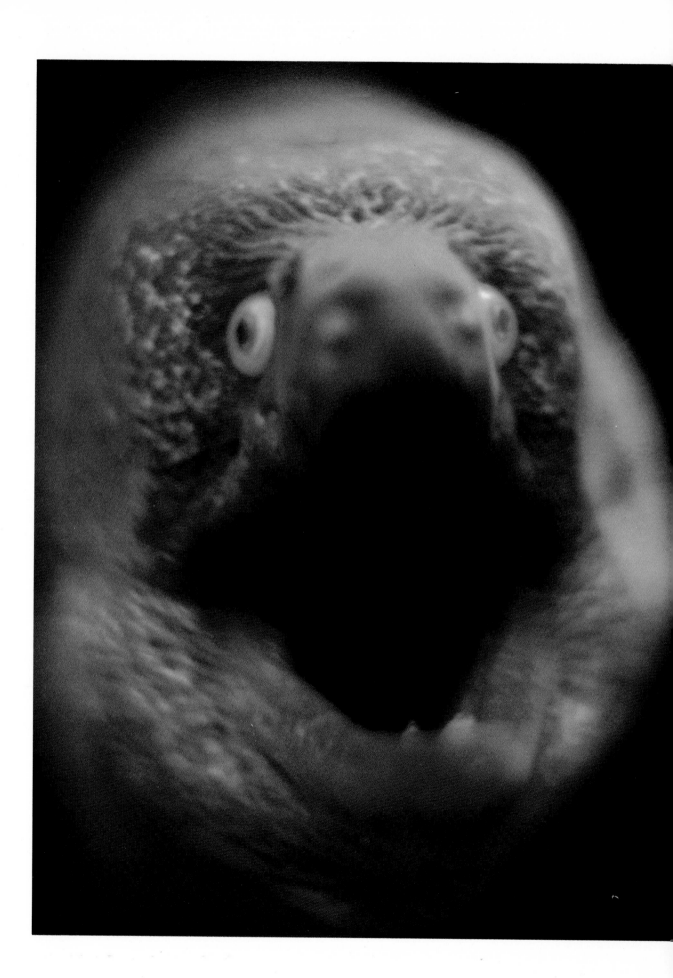

. . . night dreams .

Horses running free,
their manes flying free;
the stallion is the leader.
In my heart I am with them,
running free.

A dream is not like real life;
it's different in some way.
It's hazy, soft and unreal —
I always want to stay.
But when morning comes it's gone,
And just a thought which ends at dawn.

If I could have my own way,
I would be in a dream all day.

... and I awoke and it was true.
I saw everything. I saw sky of
roses, house of daisies, a tree
of orange, a book of apples, and
I loved it all and I lived with
it for the rest of my life.

I would especially like to express my appreciation to Janice Davis for permission to use selections from the previously unpublished poems of some of her students. Janice has taught for several years in the Mt. Diablo Unified School District in Concord, California, where she is presently teaching a Humanities and Fine Arts program for gifted children. Her enthusiasm, encouragement, and suggestions contributed greatly to the book. The poems of her students are on pages 14, 17, 18, 25, 28, 30, 32, 58, 60, 64, 68, 69, 71, 75, 77, 79, 88, 90, 92, 103, and 106.

I would also like to thank Barbara Gravelle for permission to use four poems from a collection which she edited, *Poems by Children of Point Arena and Manchester, California.* The poems and prose poems in this collection were written in a workshop arranged by Poetry in the Schools, May 1st and 3rd, 1972. Poetry in the Schools, San Francisco State University, 1600 Holloway Ave., San Francisco, California 94132 is a program which brings poets, students, and teachers together. The poems from this collection are on pages 11, 22, 35, 80, 83, and 84.

Other collections of children's writing which I have especially enjoyed are:

My Mind is an Ocean, Poems, Koans and Prophecies from Kids Seven to Twelve Years, collected by Dancing Dick. Spiritual Community Publications. Box 1080, San Rafael, California 1973 (paperback).

Stone Soup, A Journal of Children's Literature, edited by William Rubel. Published three times a year in November, February and May. Stone Soup, Box 83, Santa Cruz, California 95063.

The quotations are from the following sources:

Page	Name	Age	Country
9	Lynette Joass	12	New Zealand
	(from complete poem on page 6)		
11	Kenneth Howell	10	United States
14, 17	Johnny Goodman	11	United States
18	Jim	11	United States
21	Susan Morrison	11	Australia
22	Phillip Hill	10	United States
25	Heather Hill	9	United States
26	John Dodd	7	United States
28	Karen Johnson	9	United States
30	Ruth Fellows	9	United States
32	Rick DeRushia	9	United States
35	Lonnie	8	United States
39	Melanie Popkin	4	United States
40	David Bears Heart	14	United States
43, 45	Craig Barton	8	United States
47, 50	Akiko Sakai	7	Japan
52, 55, 56, 57	Vicky Williams	13	United States
58	Peter	8	United States
60	Celeste	10	United States
64	Elizabeth	9	United States
66	John Pearson	40	United States
68	Ronda	9	United States
69	Jill Siegmann	10	United States
71	Valerie Gilliam	11	United States
73	Josh	5	United States
75	Jane	10	United States
77	Karen de Golia	9	United States
79	Sally De Marche	10	United States
80, 83, 84	Elizabeth Zandberger	9	United States
87	Lynette Joass	12	New Zealand
	(from complete poem on page 6)		
88	Lynne McRae	9	United States
90	Louise Hillery	9	United States
92	Joe Baas	9	United States
94	Jaren Dahlstrom	30	United States
102	Photo by Karen Pearson	14	United States
103	Kim Wood	9	United States
106	Francis Ondricek	11	United States
108	Dick Link	8	United States

Many people have contributed to my life, my understanding, and the particular flow that emerged as *Begin Sweet World.* They are Liz Lamson; Anaïs Nin; my parents; Karen, my daughter; Anne Croswell, my sister; Jaren Dahlstrom,who designed the book so beautifully; Jenifer Bamberger; Chuck Morrell; Joe and Meri Ehrlich; Merrill Skrocki; Susan and Larry Boulet; Janice Davis and Dick Stoltzman.

I would like to express my appreciation again to the children who wrote the poems. They speak so eloquently.

The poet's inside
Is full of wondrous things
Like lungs full of flowers in full bloom
Hair full of bat's wings
And breast full of boast
Happiness and sad
Eyes full of dragons
And cars and lady's perfume
And fantasmagical things
A nose full of towels
Streets and boys, and girls
And a mouth that speaks
Hurt, happiness, sad, love,
Loneliness — and last but most
The truth around him.

Anne Ebersole
Age 9